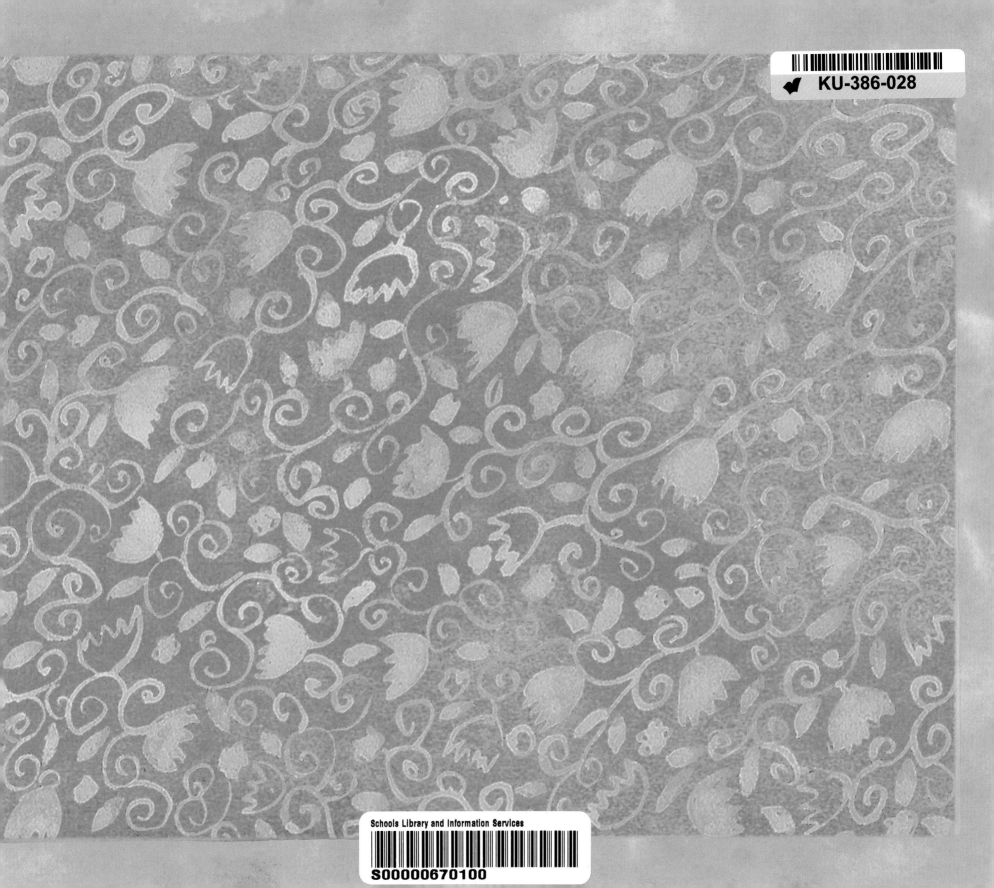

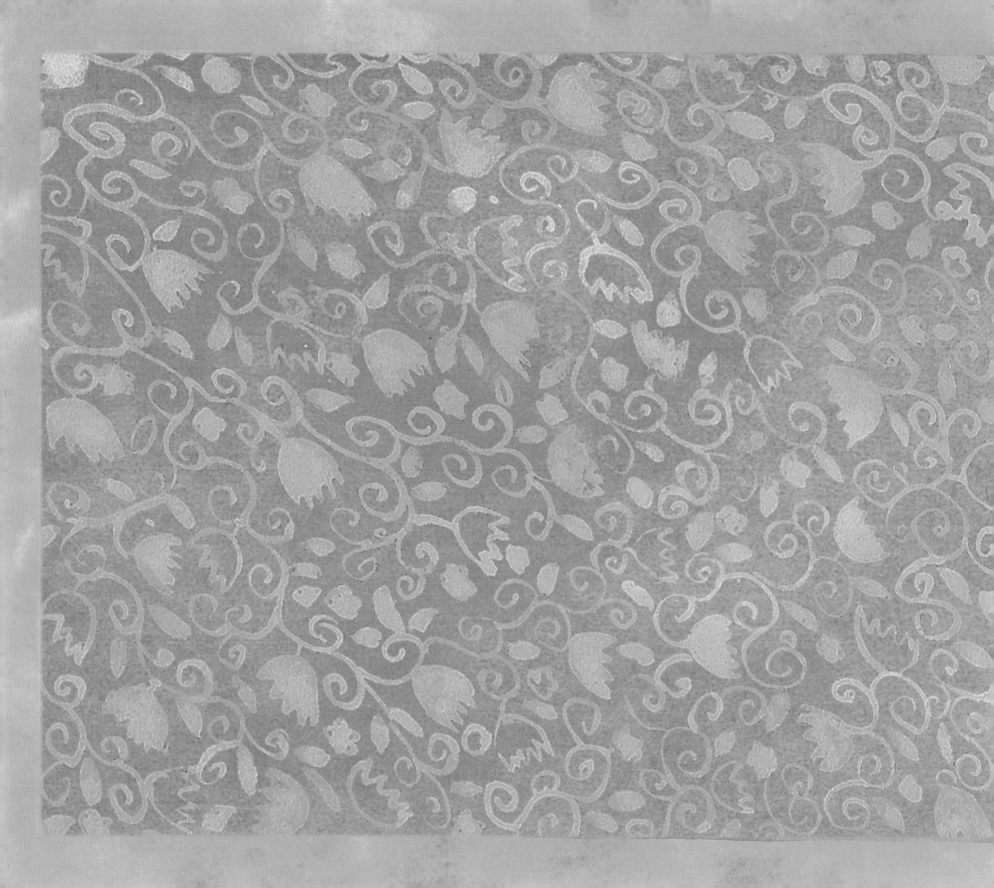

Eine Traumreise in die islamische Kunst

Journey through Islamic Art

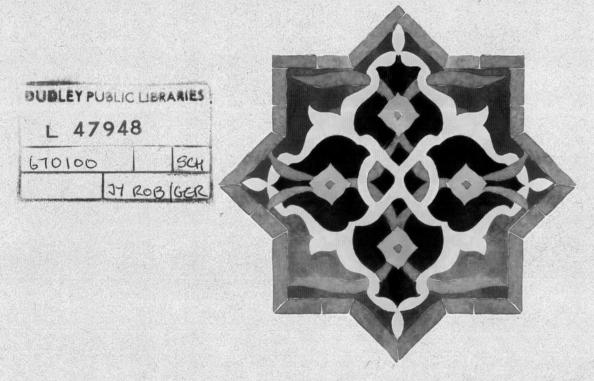

Na'ima bint Robert & Diana Mayo

mantra

Ich hörte einmal Märchen von Samarkand und Bagdad,
Von den Mogulen in Indien und den Mauren in Spanien.

*I heard tales about the cities of Samarkand and Baghdad,
About the Moghuls in India and the Moors in Spain.*

Ich sammelte silberne Fäden der Geschichten
und webte einen Fliegenden Mantel.
Der Zaubermantel brachte mich zu der
wunderbaren Welt der Kunst der Islamen.

I gathered silken threads of history in my hands and,
With them, my mind wove a flying cloak:
A cloak that took me on an amazing voyage
Through the art of the Islamic world.

Wir reisten nach Bagdad und ich sah in der alten Stadt
Moscheen, Rennbahnen, öffentliche Bäder
und lauschige Gartenhäuschen.

My cloak took me to the old city of Baghdad,
Home to mosques, public baths,
racetracks, and pavilions.

Weiter flogen wir, mein Zaubermantel und ich,
zu Wüstenschlössern, geschmückt mit Bildern
von der Decke bis zum Boden.
Dann Samara - ich bestaunte die größte
Moschee der Welt.
Ich träumte, die Gebete von den hohen Minaretten
erreichen mich in den Wolken.

Home to fortified desert castles,
Adorned with wall-paintings from floor to ceiling.
The largest mosque in the world called Samarra its home,
I imagined that the call to prayer reached me in the clouds.

Mein Zaubermantel zeigte mir Spanien,
einst ein Reich, wo sich das Morgenland
mit dem Abendland traf und Wissenschaftler,
Erfinder und Himmelsforscher die Grenzen
der menschlichen Weisheit erkundeten.

My cloak took me to Muslim Spain,
Where the East met the West.
I passed scientists, inventors and court astronomers,
Testing the limits of human knowledge.

Hier spazierte ich durch geschmückte Höfe,
vorbei an Brunnen und duftenden Gärten.

There, I wandered through ornamental courtyards,
Past fountains and scented gardens.

Hier verschmolzen
spanische und islamische
Kunst und zurück blieb
als Erbe die Al Hambra
und die große Moschee
in Cordoba.
Begierig grüßten meine
Augen die Türme,
Mosaiken und Torbögen.

The artistic heritage
of Islam and Spain
Fused to create the
Al Hambra palace and
the great mosque
of Cordoba.
Domes, mosaics and
archways greeted my
eager eyes.

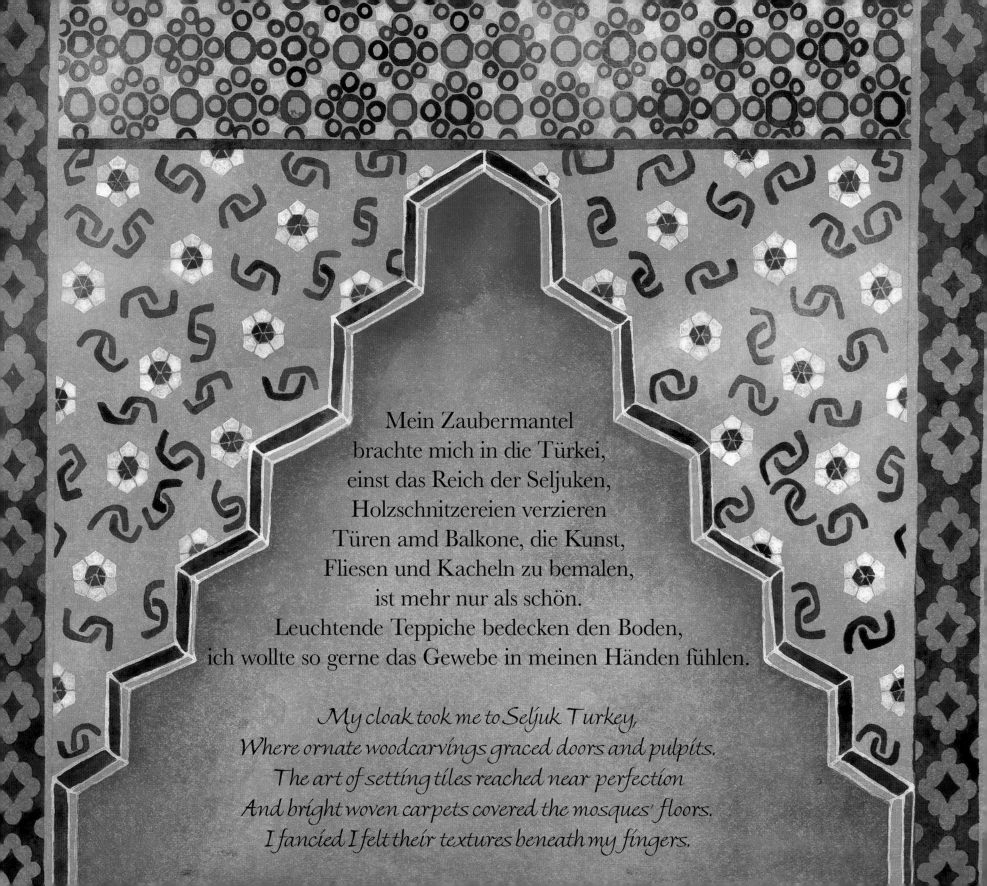

Mein Zaubermantel
brachte mich in die Türkei,
einst das Reich der Seljuken,
Holzschnitzereien verzieren
Türen amd Balkone, die Kunst,
Fliesen und Kacheln zu bemalen,
ist mehr nur als schön.
Leuchtende Teppiche bedecken den Boden,
ich wollte so gerne das Gewebe in meinen Händen fühlen.

My cloak took me to Seljuk Turkey,
Where ornate woodcarvings graced doors and pulpits.
The art of setting tiles reached near perfection
And bright woven carpets covered the mosques' floors.
I fancied I felt their textures beneath my fingers.

Mein Zaubermantel
trug mich in die Mongolei,
nach Samarkand, Land des berühmten
Nomaden, Timor der Gelähmte.
An seinem Hof versammelten sich
Künstler aus aller Welt.

*My cloak took me to the Samarkand
of Timur 'the Lame'
Where artisans from around the world
were gathered.*

Steinmetzer aus Indien,
Schreiber aus Persien,

Stonemasons from India,
calligraphers from Persia,

Silberschmiede aus der Türkei und
Seidenweber aus Damaskus.

*Silversmiths from Turkey and
silk-weavers from Damascus.*

Timor brachte sie als Gefangene,
ihre Kunst verschönerte seine Hauptstadt.
Sein Palast aber war ein Zelt,
er blieb ein Nomade bis zum Ende seines Lebens.

All brought back as captives, to beautify his city,
While his palace was a tent – a nomad to the end.

Zuletzt reisten wir,
mein Zaubermantel und ich, nach Agra.
Geräuschvolle Bazare und Straßen summten
Gerüchte vom Taj Mahal.

My cloak took me to the streets of Agra,
Where rumours of the Taj Mahal filled buzzing bazaars.

Die Legende erzählt, der Kaiser Shah Jahar
versprach seiner sterbenden Gemahlin,
ein Mausoleum zu bauen, ganz aus weißem Marmor.

A building born from a deathbed promise,
Its garment of white marble
Shimmered in the light.

المشرق

Die Mauern des Taj Mahals schimmern von
Schriftzeichen des Korans, bezaubernden
Blumenornamenten und geometrischen Mustern.
Die Dichter nennen Taj Mahal die
'leuchtende Morgendämmerung',
ein Bauwerk von vollendeter Schönheit.
Es soll nicht ein Grab sein, sondern ein Platz voller
Leben und Freude, das wünsche ich mir.

صباح الفجر

Calligraphic inscriptions from the Qur'aan,
Floral arabesques and geometric designs
all harmonised
And the poets named her 'Dawn's bright face'.
I wished its beauty could grace the living
and not enshroud the dead.

Meine Traumreise ist zuende.
Es war zwar nur Phantasie,
aber alle Stätte, die ich besucht habe,
kannst du auch noch heute bewundern.
Du mußt dir nur einen Zaubermantel weben wie ich
und dann reist auch du in diese erstaunliche Welt.

This voyage was a dream - a child's fantasy,
Though all its destinations are true.
I hope that your cloak will be spun by this tale
And that you will go there too.

Here are some explanations to help you enjoy the story:

Samarra
In the 9th century, after the foundation of Baghdad, the Caliph (ruler) moved his capital to the splendid city of Samarra. The Great Mosque was once the largest mosque in the Islamic world and rises to a height of 52 meters.

Islamic Spain was established in the 8th century by Muslims from North Africa who were known as Moors. For over three hundred years, Muslims, Christians and Jews lived together in a Golden Age when learning, art and culture flourished.

Seljuk Turkey was one of the eras in Islamic history. The Seljuks were Muslim rulers who took control of Persia and Turkey. Seljuk Turkey became the centre of excellence in weaving, ceramic painting and wood carving.

Born in the 14th century, **Timur 'the Lame'**, also known as Tamerlane, was a fierce and determined Mongol warrior who loved art. Whenever his armies invaded foreign cities, he would take care to protect the artisans and take them back to beautify his city, Samarkand.

The **Taj Mahal** was a monument built by the Mughal Emperor Shah Jahan in 1631 as a tribute to his loving wife Mumtaz Mahal. Legend says that she made him promise to build her a mausoleum more beautiful than any the world had ever seen.

Arabesque is an art form originally from Asia Minor. It was later adapted by Muslim artisans into a highly formalised form of intertwined flowers and plants.

The Qur'aan, the Muslim holy book, was revealed to the Prophet Muhammad (pbuh) by the Angel Gabriel. Its verses are often inscribed in beautiful patterns by calligraphers.

First published in 2005 by Mantra Lingua
Global House, 303 Ballards Lane, London N12 8NP
www.mantralingua.com

Text copyright © 2005 Na'ima bint Robert   Illustrations copyright © 2005 Diana Mayo
German translation by Renate Chambury
Dual language copyright © 2005 Mantra Lingua
All rights reserved

A CIP record for this book is available from the British Library.

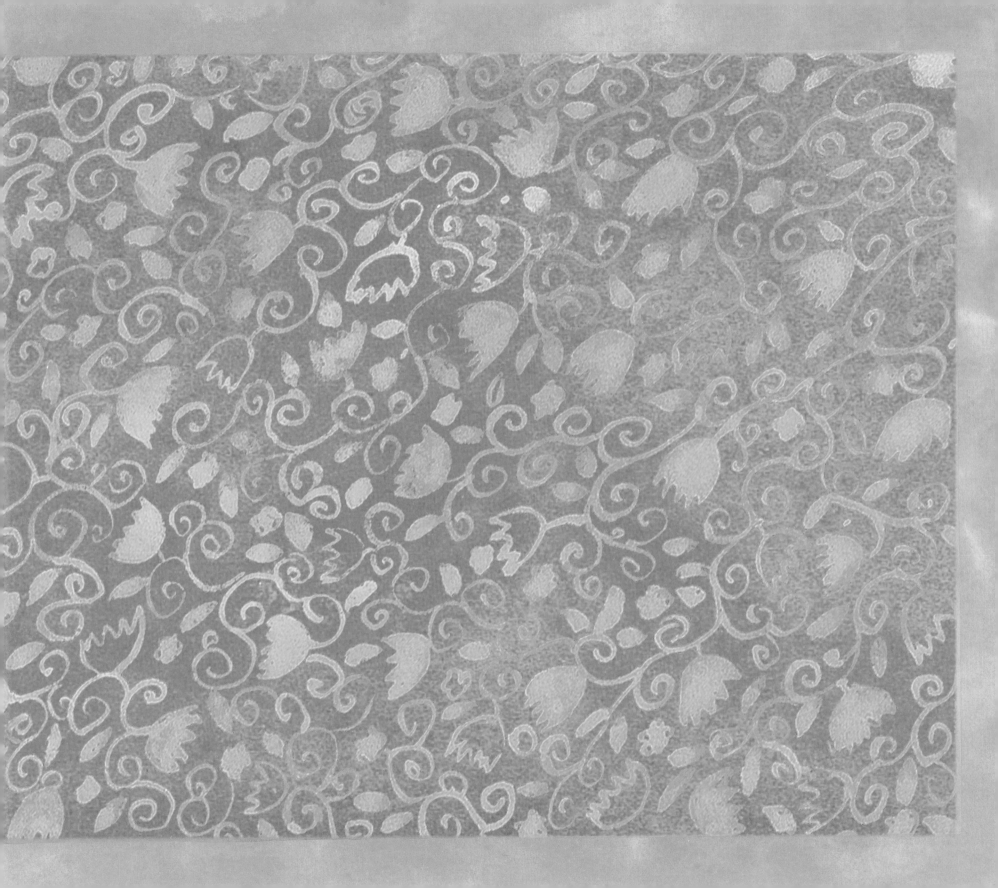

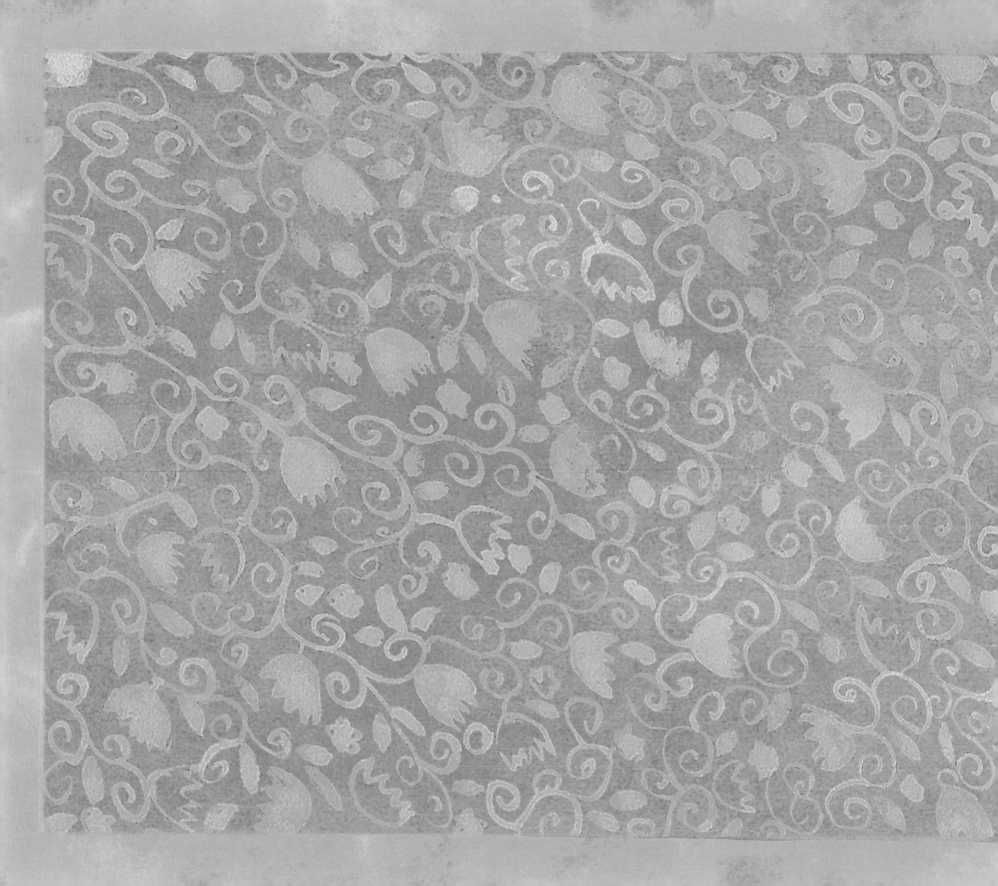